My School in the Rain Forest

How Children Attend School Around the World

Margriet Ruurs

BOYDS MILLS PRESS

HONESDALE, PENNSYLVANIA

*To the children of the world and to those who teach them:
You are the future. The possibility of peace is in your hands.*

*And with special thanks to all the children and volunteers who
shared their stories with me*

Text copyright © 2009 by Margriet Ruurs
Photographs: Credits included in acknowledgments on page 32
All rights reserved

Boyds Mills Press, Inc.
815 Church Street
Honesdale, Pennsylvania 18431
Printed in China

Library of Congress Cataloging-in-Publication Data

Ruurs, Margriet.
  My school in the rain forest : how children attend school around
the world / Margriet Ruurs. — 1st ed.
      p. cm.
  ISBN 978-1-59078-601-7 (hardcover : alk. paper)
1. Schools—Juvenile literature. 2. Students—Juvenile literature.
I. Title.

  LB1513.R88 2009
  371—dc22
                                                2009000366

First edition
The text of this book is set in 12-point Stone Serif.

10 9 8 7 6 5 4 3 2 1

CONTENTS

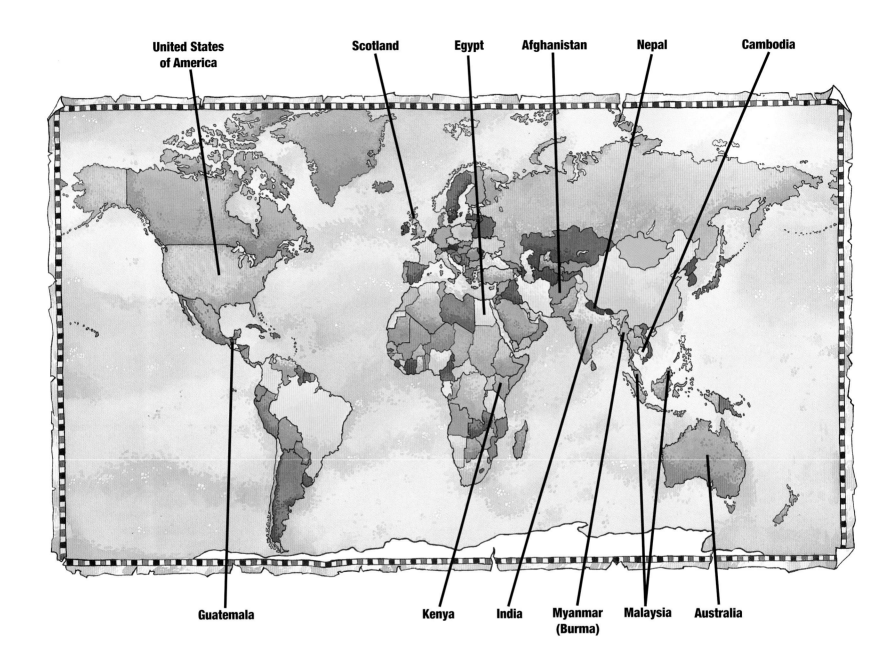

United States
of America

Scotland

Egypt

Afghanistan

Nepal

Cambodia

Guatemala

Kenya

India

Myanmar
(Burma)

Malaysia

Australia

INTRODUCTION

You live in one small spot of a very large world that you share with roughly two billion other children. Like many young people around the world, you probably attend school. Do you ever wake up wishing that you didn't have to go to school every day?

Almost all countries of the world are members of the United Nations. The purpose of the United Nations is to bring countries together to work toward peace and development and to ensure the well-being of all people. The United Nations' "Universal Declaration of Human Rights" states that "Everyone has the right to education." It further states:

Education shall be directed to the full development of the human personality and to the strengthening of respect for human rights and fundamental freedoms. It shall promote understanding, tolerance, and friendship among all nations, racial or religious groups, and shall further the activities of the United Nations for the maintenance of peace.

UNICEF, the United Nations Children's Fund, calls education "a basic human right, vital to personal and societal development and well being" and says that "all children deserve a quality education."

While some of us occasionally wish that we didn't have to go to school, it is amazing to see the many different ways in which children around the world receive an education. I attended school in The Netherlands, where there are no school buses, and my school had no library. My own children went to school in Canada's far north, where outdoor recess was cancelled only if the temperature was colder than -37 degrees Celsius or 35 degrees below zero Fahrenheit!

This book was made possible by the students, teachers, and volunteers in different parts of the world who sent me photographs and told me their stories. As a result, I learned of children in India who walk miles to school because they want to learn, and of children in Afghanistan who must face the hardships of warfare. I learned that school can be so far away that you have to live there, and that school might be in your own home. But the main lesson I learned from putting this book together is that, regardless of race or religion, children everywhere want to make friends, to learn, to read books, and to live in freedom.

Afghanistan

School Behind a Wall

The entrance to what was once the school at Shin Kalay

Students and their teacher

Years of warfare have made Afghanistan a dangerous country. Under extremely difficult conditions, some people, such as Mohammad Khan Kharoti, are determined to improve the lives of the country's children through education.

About forty years ago, Mohammad Khan Kharoti's parents were nomads, roaming the arid plains of southern Afghanistan. He didn't go to school until he was eleven years old. Learning to read and write changed his life. Now Mohammad Khan Kharoti is a medical doctor. He and his family live in the United States, but he often returns to the country of his birth to help children, just as he once was helped.

His home village of Shin Kalay sits along a winding river. *Shin Kalay* means "green village," even though the weather is hot and dry, and much of the surrounding land is dusty and brown. Shin Kalay never had a school. Mohammad Khan Kharoti wanted to change that.

After Dr. Kharoti met many times with the village elders and government officials, a plot of land was selected and the building began. The school started with eight girls and sixteen boys sitting outside on dusty ground. A few years later, more than one thousand children came to the school.

They crowded into the rooms, fifty to a class. The school held both morning and afternoon sessions to give more children a chance to attend. At first the students sat on the hard floors. But then a school in Ohio asked Dr. Kharoti if he

Noornama first went to school when she was twenty years old.

could use old desks. With help from the U.S. Army, he was able to ship nine hundred desks to Shin Kalay. "People couldn't believe that real school desks were coming," he says. "Not even the university had furniture, so how could a small village ever get desks for its students?" But the desks did arrive.

In much of Afghanistan, girls had been unable to go to school. So when Noornama enrolled in the school at Shin Kalay, she was about twenty years old. "People made fun of me when I first went to school," she says shyly, "but then they wanted to go, too!" Not only was Noornama learning math, sciences, and English, but she also started teaching the younger students in kindergarten and first grade.

A wall was built around the school, but it wasn't enough to keep out the conflict in Afghanistan. A group of armed men came and demolished the school. Though the village grieves the loss, the people are proud of what they have accomplished. More than one thousand children can now read and write. Over four hundred of these students are girls, including Noornama. Now some students have gone to attend school in Kabul and elsewhere.

One day, with the help of Dr. Kharoti, the village will build a new school. More children will come so they can learn to read and write, because the people of Shin Kalay know that education means hope.

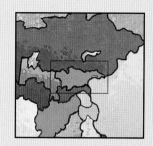

Islamic Republic of Afghanistan
Capital: Kabul
Estimated population: 32,000,000

Known as the crossroads of central Asia, Afghanistan is a landlocked country bordered by Pakistan, China, Iran, Tajikistan, Turkmenistan, and Uzbekistan. This Islamic nation's history and culture date back over five thousand years. After decades of war, the country is on the long road to recovery. The official languages are Dari, or Afghan Farsi, and Pashto. But there are more than thirty other languages and dialects spoken by various ethnic groups.

Because the school had no desks when it first opened, the students sat on the floor.

Charlie and Jorja cool off on a hot summer day.

Australia

School of the Air

The town of Alice Springs lies at the heart of Australia, far from the big cities. It gets very hot in this part of the country, which is known as the Australian outback. During the winter, which in the Southern Hemisphere lasts from May to September, clouds are rare in the skies over Alice Springs. Temperatures can be low, but the weather is usually pleasant. During the summer, from October to April, it can be as hot as 104 degrees Fahrenheit (40 degrees Celsius).

Charlie's father is a farmer who produces hay for horses, cows, goats, and even camels. Charlie and his family live about 62 miles (100 kilometers) from the town of Alice Springs, a distance too far to travel every day. So Charlie and other children across the outback attend the Alice Springs School of the Air. Originally, the school connected students and teachers by radio. Today, the school also uses the Internet. The School of the Air serves children living in parts of the Northern Territory, South Australia, and Western Australia.

Ten students make up Charlie's second-year class, but he shares his "classroom," a special schoolroom in his home, with only his little sister, Jorja, who is in preschool. When Charlie logs on to his computer, he can see his teacher on the screen, but she can't see him. The school day begins with students sharing news. When his teacher asks Charlie

Charlie, ready for class with the Alice Springs School of the Air

a question, he radios back the answer. And he can respond by writing in the chat box that appears on his computer screen. The other children in his class can also hear Charlie talking on the radio or read what he types in the chat box. Charlie says, "One of my friends lives ten hours away from me, but during our lessons by computer, I can hear him talking."

When school is off the air, Charlie's mom helps him with his schoolwork. But there are times when he also works with his teacher in person. Once a year, she tries to visit each student in his or her home. These visits are called patrol visits.

Three times a year the students of the School of the Air travel to Alice Springs to attend school together, as other kids do. "I'm so lucky we do this," says Charlie, "because we get to stay in a motel room all week. Some of my classmates stay at the same place, and after school we play and swim in the pool!" These visits are a special time for Charlie, especially when your nearest classmate lives 15 miles (24 kilometers) away.

Commonwealth of Australia
Capital: *Canberra*
Estimated population: *20,000,000*

Australia is not only a continent in the Southern Hemisphere, but it is also a country of six states and two territories. The name Australia *comes from the Latin word* australis, *which means "southern." The official language is English, but Aborigines speak more than two hundred different languages of their own.*

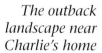

The outback landscape near Charlie's home

Charlie and Jorja

Students paddle their way to school.

Cambodia

A Floating School

In the humid heart of Cambodia, near the city of Angkor (*ang*-kor), lies Tonlé Sap (*ton*-lay sahp), the largest freshwater lake in Southeast Asia. Rivers crisscross this green, tropical region and feed into the lake. During the monsoon season, rainfall can total almost 60 inches (150 centimeters) or more. The Tonlé Sap River, which connects the lake with the Mekong River, swells so much from the rain that it reverses its flow. Water is pushed back up from the Mekong River into Tonlé Sap, expanding it to almost 6,200 square miles (16,000 square kilometers) and up to 30 feet (9 meters) deep, flooding the surrounding fields and forests.

Near the town of Siem Reap (*see*-um *ree*-up), thousands of people do not have homes on land. They live in floating houses. Life here is centered on the water. Many people make a living from fishing. Almost all transportation takes place on the river, and trading happens in small villages.

Mouen, left, is learning to read and write.

Whole villages float, going up and down with the water level. Even the school floats!

Mouen and her friends travel to their school by water. Early in the morning, they climb into their wooden boats and pick up friends on the way to school. Mouen feels fortunate to go to school. Not all families own a boat, and many children can't go to the school because they have no means to get there. Mouen is learning to count, read, and write. She is also studying the history of her country. Mouen doesn't know if she will ever leave her village, but she loves to learn about children who live in other corners of the world.

When school is out, Mouen and her classmates play traditional games. Then they climb into their boats and paddle back home.

Kingdom of Cambodia
Capital: *Phnom Penh* (pah-nahm *pen*)
Estimated population: *14,000,000*

*Cambodia is located in Southeast Asia on the coast of the Gulf of Thailand. It shares its borders with Thailand, Vietnam, and Laos. The majority of the population is Cambodian, but other ethnic groups include Chinese, Vietnamese, and Laotian. The official language is Khmer (ka-**mair**), but French and English are also spoken.*

The floating school on Tonlé Sap, a great lake in the heart of Cambodia

Learning online

Egypt

Virtual School

Outside Cairo, on the edge of the desert, is a most unusual school. In fact, the name of the school is Desert's Edge. What makes this school unusual is its method of education. Some of the teachers at the school are thousands of miles away from their students. That's because the students are learning online with teachers who live in the United States. The school believes that education should be directed by the student and that learning happens at different times, in different ways, and through life experiences. As a result, students follow individual study plans and decide what they need to do each day to accomplish their goals.

The students aren't alone, however. Actual teachers are ready to help them with online schoolwork as well as other activities. But the teachers don't stand in front of a class. At Desert's Edge, instruction may take place by the pool or in the yard or even in the horse paddock. Kristen, one of the teachers, says, "There is no typical day at this school!" Students of different ages and nationalities may work together as they learn English, history, reading, and other subjects.

Seventeen-year-old Niveen is one of the oldest students at Desert's Edge. She and her family fled Sudan and made the long, hard journey to Cairo by boat and train. They came to Egypt to escape religious persecution. Niveen's parents also wanted to give their children a better education. When

Two friends in the desert—L'abri and Niveen—with an ancient pyramid in the distance

she first arrived in Egypt, Niveen attended classes at a center for displaced children. But then she was offered the opportunity to attend Desert's Edge School. Niveen thanks her parents for making it possible.

"The thing I want most is to pay them back just a little bit for what they have done for me," Niveen says. "I want them to walk with their heads high and say, 'This is my daughter, and we are proud of her!'" One day Niveen hopes to become a doctor so that she can help others.

Eight-year-old L'abri is the youngest student at Desert's Edge. She recently trekked for three days through the mountain range of the Sinai Peninsula with her fellow students. She slept under the stars, hiked Mount Sinai, met the local Bedouin people, and learned about their culture.

Back at school, L'abri taught Niveen how to ride a bike. Learning from each other and from the world around them is what students do best at this school on the edge of the desert.

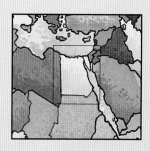

Arab Republic of Egypt
Capital: *Cairo*
Estimated population: *82,000,000*

Egypt, a nation in northern Africa, has been a unified country for more than five thousand years. It borders the Mediterranean Sea on the north, Libya on the west, the Gaza Strip and Israel on the east, and Sudan on the south. The Nile flows north through Egypt and empties into the Mediterranean, where the river spreads out to form the lush and fertile Nile Delta. The people speak Arabic, which is the official language of the country, but English and French are also spoken.

. . . and doing class projects

Time for reading new books . . .

The students of the school in Punta Arenas

Guatemala

Lessons in the Rain Forest

The Rio Dulce is a huge river that winds its way like a green snake through lush rain forest of northeast Guatemala. To get to the school of Punta Arenas (*poon*-tah ah-*ray*-nahs), children travel 6.2 miles (10 kilometers) by water. The journey begins at the main highway, where they board a boat and ride past Tikal (tee-*kahl*) National Park, which was the site of the largest city of the ancient Maya kingdom. From there, they travel up a smaller creek to a boat ramp that connects to a walkway, which passes over swamp to solid ground. *Bienvenido*, or "welcome," to Punta Arenas!

The people who live in Punta Arenas are mostly K'ichi' (kee-chay) Indians. María's home is built on stilts. The roof consists of green palm leaves. Her father is a fisherman. Her mother tends the garden, where she raises corn. From the corn, María's mother makes tortillas, which the family eats for dinner, along with fish, rice, and black beans.

Unlike the children who must travel by boat, María walks to the village school. This building, with a tin roof and large windows for ventilation, was built by volunteers of International Health Emissaries. This organization brings medical and dental care to the people of the region. It pays the salary of a teacher whom they also have helped to educate. After graduation, the teacher returned to the region to teach. The organization also gives scholarships to children

Colorful paintings on the walls of the school create a warm and welcoming atmosphere.

who are good students and encourages them to come back to their villages to teach others. Most of the parents never had the opportunity to learn to read and write, so they are happy to see their children go to school.

Juan lives a little over a mile (about two kilometers) from the village. He comes to school in his dugout canoe. Like most of his classmates, Juan loves to play soccer at recess. After school, Juan and other children board their boats for the journey home.

Republic of Guatemala
Capital: *Guatemala City*
Estimated population: *13,000,000*

This small, mountainous country is located in Central America, between the Pacific Ocean and Caribbean Sea. The land was once home to the great Mayan civilization, which flourished throughout the surrounding region between AD 250 and 900. Today, more than half of Guatemalans are descendants of the Maya. Most of the people speak Spanish, but twenty-three native languages are spoken as well.

Children travel a little more than six miles to attend school.

María

India

School in the Jungle

Saritha (right) takes a walk near her village with her mother and brother.

Along with about seven hundred other students, Saritha and Vipin attend school in Neyyardam, a village in the southern state of Kerala, India. Saritha and Vipin walk almost two miles (three kilometers) to and from school every day. Their school is a spot in the jungle with a smooth dirt floor sheltered by walls of lush green plants.

Neyyardam is surrounded by beautiful hills and forests. People build their homes with mud bricks and make roofs from palm leaves.

The school, however, does not have a roof. During monsoon season, the students often huddle together under umbrellas or seek shelter in a nearby hut. When the rains have passed, the students sit on plastic sheets spread over the mud floor.

School is free in India, but most people in this area are too poor to buy the required school uniforms, pens, or books. The children are often needed at home to earn a living or work in the fields. Saritha and Vipin attend a school that is run by a volunteer organization. It provides free supplies, clothing, and food for the children in this area.

Saritha is fourteen years old. Girls don't always receive an education in India, but Saritha hopes to be a nurse one day. She walks a long way to school. When class begins, she

Saritha (right) with her sisters at school.

sits with her classmates on a mat that covers the dirt floor. The blackboard is balanced against a chunk of cement wall. It's not unusual for a cow or chickens to wander through the "classroom." When classes are finished for the day, Saritha returns home to help her mother clean the house. After the family meal, she says her prayers, and goes to bed around 10:00 p.m. Saritha needs her rest before the long walk back to school in the morning.

Vipin is thirteen years old. His favorite subject is social studies. Vipin dreams of becoming a pilot when he grows up. After he returns home from school, Vipin gathers leaves to feed the family goat, which provides milk and cheese.

Vipin and Saritha like going to school to learn new things. Since they live so far away from other villages, school is a great place for them to meet and play with their friends.

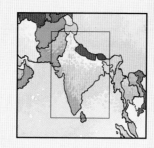

Republic of India
Capital City: *New Delhi*
Estimated population: *1,140,000,000*

India's civilization dates back to 2500 BC, making it one of the oldest in the world. This vast land has a variety of landscapes, with the Himalayas in the north, deserts in the west, rolling plains along the Ganges River, and coastlines on the Arabian Sea and Bay of Bengal. The official language is Hindi, but English is also common. And there are fourteen other languages spoken in India, including Bengali, Urdu, Tamil, and Punjabi.

The children and their teacher enjoy playing games.

Vipin solves a problem on the blackboard.

Halima

Kenya

School Under a Tree

Maweni is a small village on the southern coast of Kenya. About four hundred people live here. Their homes are one-room, five-foot-square huts thatched together with leaves. Everything they own fits into these huts. The village is poor, and parents cannot afford to send their children to schools in nearby towns. Many of the adults don't know how to read or write or even how to hold a pencil. But the children of Maweni are eager to learn. Education may help to improve their lives.

Halima used to attend school in the open air under a tree, which provided shade for the children. But thanks to volunteers and local teachers, the "school under a tree" is now enclosed. Instead of sitting on the ground, Halima and her schoolmates sit on benches. Classes are still out-of-doors because the walls and roof are open. Sometimes the children chase chickens out of the school before lessons can start.

Children come to learn, sing, and eat nutritious food. Halima brings her siblings to school so they can enjoy rice for lunch, too. The school has few teaching supplies. For instance, the students use sticks and stones for counting lessons. The students have few books as well. When they receive a book, Halima and her friends read it together, and each student eagerly awaits his or her chance to turn the page.

While the children are in school, their mothers make

gravel. They chip away at quartz to make smaller chunks. During recess, the children help their mothers. Selling gravel provides a small income for the people of the village.

Even though tribal war makes life difficult in the area, the different religious groups in Maweni live in peace. Christian children say Muslim prayers, while their Muslim friends sing carols at Christmas. When life is tough, the people of Maweni lift their spirits by singing. The school uses song to teach the children about colors, counting, language, and much more. The singing voices of children often fill the air around the school, joining that of the birds in nearby trees.

Recently, volunteers took Halima and her classmates on a school bus for a field trip. She and the children from Maweni had never seen the world outside their village. The experience gave them both courage and hope for a better future.

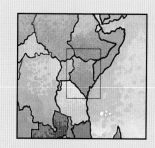
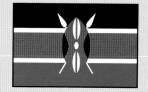

Republic of Kenya
Capital: *Nairobi*
Estimated population: *38,000,000*

The Republic of Kenya is located in East Africa. The country takes its name from Mount Kenya, the highest mountain in Kenya and the second-highest in Africa, after Mount Kilimanjaro. Mount Kenya is situated in Mount Kenya National Park, one of the many parks and wildlife reserves in Kenya that draw tourists from all corners of the world. Kenya, a culturally diverse country with forty-two different tribes, has two official languages, English and Kiswahili.

Time for recess

A mother of the village chips quartz for extra income.

Malaysia

An International School

Corim

International schools are private schools where children from many countries receive an education. Classes are usually taught in English. The parents of the students often work for international organizations, large companies, embassies, or missionary programs that require them to live abroad. Local children also can attend these schools to improve their English. Visiting students and their families live in the host country only for a few years before moving again. There are hundreds of international schools around the world. While some international schools are small, others have hundreds of students from many different countries.

Corim attends Mont'Kiara International School in Kuala Lumpur, Malaysia. Born in the Philippines, Corim has also lived in Ho Chi Minh City, Vietnam. He rides a school bus to the international school, where he is in fifth grade. His day begins by sitting in a community circle with his fellow students to share stories. After math comes recess, which is Corim's favorite part of the day. He loves to play soccer (or football, as it is called here). During lunch, the students at Mont'Kiara eat together in a large cafeteria. Outside the school windows, they may see monkeys dangling from the branches of tropical trees or colorful birds perched among the blossoms. In world

The school library has more than sixteen thousand books.

language class, Corim and his fellow students study Spanish or French. Corim speaks both English and Tagalog, a language of the Philippines. His best friends are from Denmark, Canada, and the Philippines. "Sometimes it makes me a little sad to move again," says Corim, "especially when I don't know anyone at my new school. But it is also exciting to discover new places and to make new friends.

"One of my favorite days at school is National Day," Corim continues. "We all dress in the traditional clothing of our own country, and we get a 'passport' to visit other classrooms, which are decorated as different countries. It's a fun way to learn about different cultures and their customs."

Occasionally, students from Mont'Kiara go on a field trip. Some of the children recently attended a mock United Nations congress in The Hague, The Netherlands.

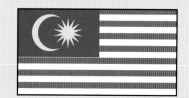

Malaysia
Capital: *Kuala Lumpur (kwah-lah* loom*-poor)*
Estimated population: *26,000,000*

Malaysia is located in Southeast Asia. The country includes two regions—West Malaysia and East Malaysia—which are divided by the South China Sea. It is a multicultural society whose population includes Malays (the largest ethnic group), Chinese, Indians, and others. Malay is the official language, although many people also speak English and various Chinese dialects, as well as Tamil and indigenous languages such as Iban and Kadazan.

Part of the school grounds

Corim and his friends from different nations stand at the entrance of Mont'Kiara.

Myanmar (Burma)

School in a Monastery

Ma Thu Zar Moe, a young Buddhist nun

Rajgir Monastery School is part of a Buddhist monastery located outside Yangon, the capital city of Myanmar. Most of the people of Myanmar practice Theravada (ther-ah-*vah*-dah) Buddhism, the oldest form of Buddhism. Traditionally, the poor of Myanmar find help through Buddhist monasteries, such as the one that operates the Rajgir School. Approximately five hundred children attend the school. Some are orphans who live at the monastery. Others live in the surrounding area.

Classes at the school can be large, with as many as fifty students. In some classrooms children sit on benches, while in others they sit on the floor. These classrooms are simple and bare. There are almost no teaching materials such as maps, posters, or even books.

In this culture, it is common for people to serve at a monastery at some point in their lives. They are free to leave when they wish. During this time, they are educated and serve their community. Some of the children who live at the monastery have chosen to become monks or nuns.

Ma Thu Zar Moe is fourteen years old and in the seventh grade. Her name means "beautiful rain" in Burmese. For three years, she lived at the monastery as a nun until the monastery ran out of room. Though she has moved back home with her family, Ma Thu Zar Moe still attends Rajgir Monastery School and is still a nun. Home is a hut with thatched walls and roof and a wooden floor. There is no water or electricity.

At the monastery, children learn to help others. Some of the children had suffered from skin disease, which they had contracted from washing, bathing, and sometimes drinking pond water. "I had a very happy feeling," Ma Thu Zar Moe says, "when I gave medicine to the little monks and nuns in my school group." The medicine helped to clear up the rash. Through the kindness of others, Ma Thu Zar Moe and her schoolmates at the monastery school now have a new pump, clean water, soap, and, for the first time, towels.

Union of Myanmar (MEE-n-mar), formerly known as Burma
Capital: *Yangon, formerly known as Rangoon*
Estimated population: *47,000,000*

Myanmar, also known as Burma, is a country in Southeast Asia, bordered by India in the northwest and China in the northeast. The Andaman Sea and the Bay of Bengal are to the south and west. Other neighbors are Bangladesh, Laos, and Thailand. Languages include Burmese and those of other ethnic minorities.

Ma Thu Zar Moe's parents outside their home

Students play games during recess.

*Amita, whose village is miles away,
lives at the school.*

Nepal

A Community School

Namaste (nam-ah-stay), or "welcome," to Bhattidanda
(bah-*tee*-dahn-dah), Nepal. Here in the shadows of the
Himalayas is Himaljyoti (himul-*jo*-tee) Community School. In
Nepali, *Himaljyoti* means "light of the Himalayas." The village
chose the name because the residents hope their school will
be a shining light for other schools in Nepal. Most people
living here belong to an ethnic group called Tamang. Many
are excellent mountaineers, which is a helpful skill in this part
of the world. Bhattidanda is located 5,000 feet (1,500 meters)
above sea level and 124 miles (200 kilometers)—a rough, two-
day journey—from Mount Everest.

Himaljyoti Community School is a nonprofit,
nongovernment community school, the first of its kind in
Nepal. The school was started by two people from England
with the help of the Saga Charitable Trust, an organization
that helps poor communities in undeveloped countries.
Once the school was built, it was turned over to the people
of Bhattidanda. The building serves not only as a school but
as a community center and a medical clinic.

Most of the people in Bhattidanda work hard for a
living, earning slightly more than a dollar a day.

Himaljyoti Community School, set high in the Himalayas

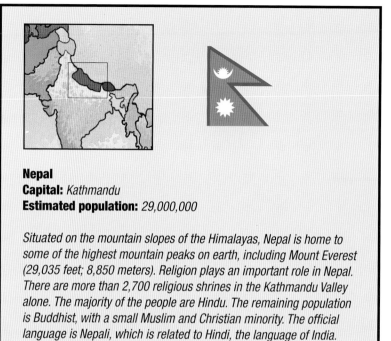

Nepal
Capital: *Kathmandu*
Estimated population: *29,000,000*

Situated on the mountain slopes of the Himalayas, Nepal is home to some of the highest mountain peaks on earth, including Mount Everest (29,035 feet; 8,850 meters). Religion plays an important role in Nepal. There are more than 2,700 religious shrines in the Kathmandu Valley alone. The majority of the people are Hindu. The remaining population is Buddhist, with a small Muslim and Christian minority. The official language is Nepali, which is related to Hindi, the language of India. A dozen other languages are spoken in Nepal as well.

Many children must work to help the family earn a living. Sending children to school costs money. They need shoes, clothing, books, even paper and pencils. The Saga Charitable Trust provides funds for school supplies and books, and people around the world can also sponsor a child directly through the trust. But the citizens of Bhattidanda are responsible for their school. They try to convince more parents to let their children come to learn.

Amita's father is a farmer in a small village with about twenty houses. At home, Amita has six brothers and six sisters. She feels lucky to attend Himaljyoti Community School, even though it means living away from her family. Since her village is about four miles (six kilometers) away from school, Amita lives with her uncle and his family in Bhattidanda. Less than 35 percent of women in Nepal can read or write. That's why it's important that girls like Amita are given a chance to go to school. One day Amita hopes to read to her own children and encourage them to attend school and learn to read and write as well.

An upper-grade classroom at Himaljyoti Community School

Scotland

Boarding School in a Castle

Ruairidh in his dorm room

Imagine living at your school all day and night. Merchiston Castle School in Edinburgh, Scotland, is a boarding school for boys founded over 175 years ago. In 1833, the school was housed in a fifteenth-century castle. Today, the school's campus has many buildings and is located not far from the original site.

Ruairidh (*roh*-ree) is twelve years old. Even though his home is less than an hour away, he lives at the school full time along with over three hundred other boys. Some of the boys are from homes that are much farther away. Some students even come from different countries. Ruairidh lives in a building called Pringle. It has six dorm rooms, plus rooms with a pool table, Ping-Pong table, and Foosball table.

The school places great emphasis on community spirit. Students and teachers, some of whom also live at the school, share meals together in the dining hall and sometimes attend formal dinners in the Old Library.

History is a living part of Merchiston Castle School's heritage. The school continues to observe a number of Scottish traditions. For example, bagpipes are often played, and on special occasions, the students wear kilts. For classes, the boys wear a school uniform. Merchiston Castle School may seem like a formal place, but Ruairidh enjoys it here. One of his favorite buildings is Gibson House, the school's Science Department. Ruairidh loves science. He says, "There are loads of experiments to do!"

During his free time, he plays soccer, cricket, and rugby with his classmates. The annual rugby match between Merchiston Castle School and Edinburgh Academy, another independent school, has been played for over 150 years. To Ruairidh, a boarding school is never a boring school.

A centuries-old ruin on the grounds of Merchiston Castle School

Scotland
Capital: *Edinburgh*
Estimated population: 5,000,000

Scotland lies to the north of England. It is one of the countries that comprise the United Kingdom of Great Britain and Northern Ireland. Along with the mainland, Scotland consists of more than 790 islands.

Boys in their uniforms outside one of the old school buildings on campus

Victoria and Jessica

United States of America

A Home School

In a green valley among farm fields and tall oak trees lies the small town of Shedd in Oregon. Twelve-year-old Jessica and her family live on a farm just outside the town. Jessica's home is also her school. Like an estimated one million children in the United States, she and her brothers and sister are homeschooled.

The school day starts around 8:00 a.m. The family uses one room of their house as a schoolroom. The children sit around a table with their teacher, who is also their mother. Math, vocabulary, Latin, and science are all on Jessica's daily schedule. Physical education class is also held every day. Jessica's mother drives the children to a gym where they meet other homeschoolers in the area.

Jessica has never attended a public school. She likes being schooled at home. "We never get sent to the principal when we get into trouble!" she says, laughing. Like all homeschoolers, Jessica must take yearly tests to make sure she is academically on track.

Jessica's home is her school.

When school is at home, it is hard to separate learning from other responsibilities. For example, Jessica and her siblings raise goats and chickens. They sell the animals to earn money for college. Harrison, Jessica's older brother, drives the tractor and works on a neighboring farm during the summer.

The outdoors is another type of classroom. While learning about the indigenous people who once lived here, the kids explore the woods, looking for arrowheads. For a science lesson, they catch polliwogs in the creek and study their life cycle.

Like kids who attend public school, Jessica is involved in after-school and weekend activities. She loves her ballet lessons. That's one of the places where she meets her friends and other kids. Victoria, Jessica's fourteen-year-old sister, celebrated her last birthday with a sleepover. She and twelve friends slept in the hayloft.

Besides spending a lot of time outside on the farm, Jessica and her family love to read. Rather than watch television, they curl up with some good books. One of Jessica's favorites? *Little House on the Prairie.*

United States of America
Capital: *Washington, D.C.*
Estimated population: *303,000,000*

The United States of America is located in North America, bordered by Canada in the north and Mexico in the south. It includes two states that are separated from the mainland: Alaska, in the northwest, and Hawaii, in the Pacific Ocean. Its population is one of the most ethnically diverse in the world. English is the main language.

Jessica and Victoria with one of their chickens

Harrison works on the farm.

World

School on a Ship

The children of Mercy Ship Academy

Imagine your classroom had portholes for windows and constantly sailed around the world. The MV *Anastasis* is a hospital ship, operated by Mercy Ships, a global charity that brings free health care to people in developing countries. Many people live and work onboard the ship. Their children attend Mercy Ship Academy.

Rebekka is nine years old and in grade 4. Her brother Steffan is thirteen years old and in grade 7. They have spent most of their lives onboard the ship. Their father is the captain and their mother works in the ship's offices. Steffan says, "When you are quietly reading, you can hear the ropes of the ship creaking as you bob on the waves of the Indian Ocean. And at recess you can see dolphins!"

The entire length of the ship is about 150 yards, not much larger than a football field. Imagine sharing that space with your family and all of your neighbors, friends, and teachers.

Rebekka has only three other classmates in her grade. She has visited Spain, France, Sweden, Iceland, Norway, Ghana, Liberia, Gambia, and many other countries. When Rebekka, Steffan, and their parents are not on the ship, they stay on the Faroe Islands in the North Atlantic Ocean or visit their grandparents in the United States. So it is no wonder that Rebekka's favorite subject is geography.

Rebekka

The kids do homework in their own cabin or in the ship's library. They like to hang out on the pool deck. Sometimes the students leave the ship for a field trip to an island or to explore a new shore. They like to play on beaches.

They study all the regular school subjects, in addition to the Bible, and help on the ship. As a hospital ship, the MV *Anastasis* has a patients' ward on one of the decks. The children often "adopt" patients to play with, to help them, and to pray for them. Steffan says, "I recently hung out with a boy called Reuben. He was twelve years old and had horrible burns on his face from falling into a fire when he was little. Reuben was on the ship for reconstructive surgery to his face. We had so much fun together. I taught him to play Uno, and he ended up always beating me!" At first, Steffan says, he was shocked to see patients, but now he is used to it and likes to help them feel at home during their time on the ship.

Both kids like to play basketball and soccer during their physical education class. "But," Rebekka laughs, "sometimes we lose balls overboard!" So next time you find a ball on a beach—who knows—it might have come from a school on a ship.

Earth is almost 197 million square miles (510.044 million square kilometers) in size. Of this, 57.50 square miles (149.5 million square kilometers) is land and 139.43 square miles (362.518 million square kilometers) is water; 70.8 percent of the world's surface is water, 29.2 percent is land. There are 194 countries in the world and four oceans: the Pacific, Atlantic, Arctic, and the Indian oceans. The lowest point on Earth is the Mariana Trench: 36,198 feet (11,033 meters) below the surface of the Pacific Ocean. The highest point on Earth is Mount Everest at 29,035 feet (8,850 meters). There are close to seven billion people on Earth, including about 2.2 billion children.

Reuben, Steffan, and a bright balloon in the patients' ward

The MV Anastasis *docked at one of its many ports of call.*

ACKNOWLEDGMENTS

I could not have compiled this book without the help of many people who kindly shared stories and photos:

Afghanistan: Mohammad Khan Kharoti and Yama Kharoti, and courtesy of Green Village Schools

Australia: Nicole Buddle

Cambodia: Barbara Ledig Sheehan, Photo Angkor Journey; Teresita S. de Guzman, R.N.

Egypt: Juleen and Roger Keevy

Guatemala: Ted Holcombe, Asociación Rescate; John Faia, International Health Emissaries; Dr. Joe Jensen, Dr. Terri Lisagor, Mari Hammon

India: Brenda and Brian Luzader

Kenya: Brenda and Brian Luzader

Malaysia: Mont'Kiara International School, Kuala Lumpur: Laurie Collins, Robert Carrelli

Myanmar (Burma): Iris Mennie

Nepal: SAGA Charitable Trust, United Kingdom; Tom and Barbara Lowen

Scotland: Gayle Cordiner, courtesy of Merchiston Castle School

United States of America: Kathi Winter; photos by Margriet Ruurs

World: Mercy Ship MV *Anastasis*: Lucy-Anne Mizen, Debra Bell, Esther Biney, Mercy Ships International

A special thank-you to all the children who allowed me a glimpse into their everyday life.

References:
United Nations Universal Declaration of Human Rights
Facts and population figures from the United Nations Children's Fund (UNICEF), the Central Intelligence Agency World Factbook (www.cia.gov/library/publications/the-world-factbook/) and U.S. Department of State

To learn more about the schools and their sponsors, visit www.margrietruurs.com and click on the title of this book.